Remembering The Light
Through Prosetry*

(*An Integration of
Prose and Poetry)

Remembering The Light
Through Prosetry*

(*An Integration of
Prose and Poetry)

ANDY PETRO

Outskirts Press, Inc.
Denver, Colorado

The opinions expressed in this manuscript are solely the opinions of the author and do not represent the opinions or thoughts of the publisher. The author has represented and warranted full ownership and/or legal right to publish all the materials in this book.

Remembering The Light Through Prosetry
(*Integrating Prose And Poetry)
All Rights Reserved.
Copyright © 2011 Andy Petro
v2.0

Cover Photo © 2011 Andy Petro. All rights reserved - used with permission.

This book may not be reproduced, transmitted, or stored in whole or in part by any means, including graphic, electronic, or mechanical without the express written consent of the publisher except in the case of brief quotations embodied in critical articles and reviews.

Outskirts Press, Inc.
http://www.outskirtspress.com

ISBN: 978-1-4327-7593-3

Outskirts Press and the "OP" logo are trademarks belonging to Outskirts Press, Inc.

PRINTED IN THE UNITED STATES OF AMERICA

Contents

Acknowledgments i

Prologue iii

CHAPTER 1: The Event 1
Death by Drowning and Back Again 9

CHAPTER 2: Remembering Eternity 11
Being In The Light ... A Love Experience 14

CHAPTER 3: Early Childhood Visions 17
Childhood Visions 20

CHAPTER 4: Breathing In The Present Moment 23
The Moment Is Now 30

CHAPTER 5: We Are All Pieces Of The Light 33
Pieces of God ... Pieces of Light 35

CHAPTER 6: Vibrations Remembered 37
Vibrations 39

CHAPTER 7: What Is Unconditional Love? 41
Unconditional Love 43

CHAPTER 8: Why Not Try Love? 45
Give Love A Chance 47

CHAPTER 9: Creating Random Acts Of Joy 49
Random Acts Of Joy 51

CHAPTER 10: Who Is A True Friend? 53
A True Friend 55

CHAPTER 11: How Many Choices? 57
Three Choices 59

CHAPTER 12: Touch—An Awesome Dream 61
Touch 63

CHAPTER 13: What Does It Mean To Be Human? 65
To Be Human 67

CHAPTER 14: Cancer And The Light 69
A Love Poem To Cancer 71

CHAPTER 15: What If I Could Meet Me Again? 73
If I Could Meet Me Again 75

CHAPTER 16: Who Am I—Really? 77
Who Am I? 79

CHAPTER 17: And I'm Remembering Again 81
And I Remember 83

CHAPTER 18: How Does It Feel To Be Back? 85
How Does It Feel? 86

CHAPTER 19: Death And The Light 89
A Love Poem To Death 91

CHAPTER 20: Finally, Returning To The Light 93
Return To The Light 99

Epilogue 101

Acknowledgments

FOR OVER 25 YEARS, I have wanted to write about my Near Death Experience. All of my previous attempts have been aborted or destroyed after completion. Those attempts did not describe the essence of my experience. I couldn't find the three-dimensional words that would adequately describe my journey into a multidimensional universe. So I quit!

The first person I discussed the in-depth details of my earth-death experience with was Bob Becker, a close and trusted friend. He kept urging me to write my memories down so others could feel and experience them as well. Bob, I thank you for your persistence, and not giving up on me.

A few years ago I joined a local writers group and shared my previous writing disappointments with the group. We eventually came up with the concept of using both prose and poetry to describe my adventures on the other side. I am very grateful to three special writers in the group: Alan Lowe, Jim Fulcomer, and Sue Fone. Thank you all for your encouragement to pursue and complete my book of "prosetry."

The first person to edit my work was a long-time business

associate and friend, Anita Rae. She took my first draft and gave it form and substance. Thank you, Anita.

My two daughters-in-law, Michelle and Julie Petro, both helped in getting the book into its final form and I am thankful for their assistance.

Melissa Gratiot did the final edit of my book. She gave it the finishing touches and I am very thankful for her kind words and great editing.

I was fortunate to have ongoing support from my wonderful wife, Doris. She assisted me with ideas and suggestions throughout the entire process. Doris, thank you for always being there for me.

Prologue

I WAS IN PURE ECSTASY. From the moment I let go of my struggle to stay alive and drowned, I experienced the true meaning of ecstasy.

I was propelled into a tunnel moving toward the Light. I could feel a cosmic breeze on my face. I knew all my physical sensations were still with me, but much more intense. It was as if my nerve endings were rubbed with sandpaper and all my senses became ultra receptive. I instantly felt a warm sensation surge throughout my entire body; like walking into a warm room after being out in an ice-cold snowstorm. When I looked at the Light I could feel its brightness on my retinas. Amazingly, I didn't feel any pain from the intense Light; even though it was thousands of times brighter than the sun—I didn't even squint. The painful ringing in my ears was suddenly gone, as if someone had turned off a screeching fire alarm.

I remember being suspended in mid-space, hovering before the Light. I was filled with a warmth and peace that completely consumed me. I was looking directly into the Light's face and I remembered it from some distant past. I was enthralled by its majestic beauty and radiance. When the

Light said, "Andy, do not be afraid," "Andy, I love you," and "Andy, we love you," I remembered that I was home again. We were so happy together, the Light, all the other surrounding Lights, and me.

I sensed a complete openness and delight between the Light and me. There was nothing I ever did that the Light didn't know and accept. The Light acknowledged all my experiences without any judgment or condemnation. I'm accepted for who I am...and I am Andy. I am a piece of the Light, and we are all One.

My poetry writing started with a sequence of bizarre, early morning happenings. I would wake up in the middle of the night, fully alert—with strange phrases, concepts, and images spinning around in my mind. There was nothing I could do to make those mental images go away and allow me to go back to sleep. They wouldn't stop. In addition, along with these unusual thoughts and images, I sensed, for the first time in my life, an irresistible impulse to write.

I am not a writer. I don't like to write. But at each nocturnal incident I would find myself sitting at my desk, writing simple poetry that flowed from my subconscious out through the end of my pencil point. It was as if I were viewing a large chalkboard in my head constantly being filled with words, phrases, and images, which I copied down on a pad of paper. After an hour or so, I would be finished, very tired, and go back to sleep. When I awoke in the morning and read the poem I had written a few hours earlier, I was always very surprised at the poetry coming from me. Until finally, I realized the poems were not coming *from* me but rather *through* me. They were actually coming from the Light, and all I was doing was transcribing my personal experiences with the Light into poetry.

After many years, I began to realize the purpose for these nocturnal poems was to assist me in remembering, understanding, and explaining the otherwise indescribable experiences of my Near Death Experience (NDE). After many additional years, I decided to put them all together in a book for my family, friends, and anyone else interested in the remembrances from someone who died, went into the Light, and returned (unwillingly) to earth for a while. This is my story based on my personal recollections…memories of the Light that refuse to go away.

CHAPTER 1

The Event

A FEW DAYS BEFORE MY HIGH SCHOOL GRADUATION, in the summer of 1955, I experienced an unusual, frightening, and incredible event. The memory of this event is not only crystal clear, but it remains intact, exactly as it happened. Every thought, word, image, action, and feeling of this memory abides unchanged in my mind, thoughts, and soul. I have spent years trying to forget, but I always remember, and I always remember the event as if it happened today.

I am filled with joy and excitement. In a few days I will finally graduate from high school and move forward with my life. Our class decided to have a picnic at a nearby lake as our final outing before graduation, and I'm excited about going.

I arrive at the lake and it is a great day for a picnic. The sun is shining and the sky is painted a beautiful shade of blue, dotted with perfect cotton-ball clouds. A warm breeze blows the fresh smell of the trees, sand, and lake everywhere.

◀ REMEMBERING THE LIGHT THROUGH PROSETRY*

I change into my swimsuit and begin the party with some beach games before lunch. After I eat, some of my friends swim out to a floating platform about one hundred yards off shore. Once they get to the platform, they wave and yell for me to join them. The water is much too cold for me to ease in slowly, so from 20 feet back, I take a running leap and hit the water in a gigantic belly flop. My body warms a bit as I get into my swimming rhythm. Then about halfway to the floating platform, I feel the first cramping pains in my stomach and groin. *The cramps aren't that bad,* I tell myself, *and besides, I'm almost halfway there. I can make it.*

With every stroke the cramps and pain increase, and my knees buckle into my stomach. I can no longer kick my legs or straighten my body. I'm terrified! My arms move, and I don't go anywhere but down. As I struggle beneath the surface I start gagging on the water. It's in my nose, down my windpipe, and in my lungs…I'm sinking.

As I struggle, I finally get my head up out of the water. Frantically, I search the water's surface for the platform and my friends. No one recognizes my dilemma. Down I go again, deeper than before. My arms feel frozen in place and every muscle in my body screams with pain. I never imagined I could experience such unbearable pain. I sink deeper as the dazzling June sunlight fades to blackness. *Oh my God, it's all black, I can't see anything!* A loud, painful, ringing sound is in my head. It feels as if someone is sticking an ice pick in my ears. I'm convinced my brain will explode any second. I'm falling endlessly down this freezing black hole. My body trembles uncontrollably in the frigid water.

THE EVENT

I continue to sink into this ice-cold black hole; it seems to last forever. *Wait, I feel something. It's the slimy, cold weeds at the bottom of the lake.* Struggling in this tangle of weeds feels like I'm falling into an arctic snake pit. Finally I hit the bottom. I try to push myself up with trembling, numb hands, but the goo at the lake bottom holds me down and sucks me deeper into the mud. Then, I hear a strange voice inside my head say, *Andy, rest for just a moment; you need to let go.* I reply, *No, I can't, I have to get to the surface for some air.* Then the voice says again, *If you let go for just a moment, then I promise that you can return to the struggle.* I respond, *Do you promise?* And the voice answers back, *Yes, I promise.*

In my frozen panic state I say to myself, *All right then, okay then, I'll stop for just a moment of rest.*

I stop struggling. I let go…

The very instant I let go, I am hurled into a dark, black tunnel. I look back and somehow, I can see my body stuck in the weeds at the bottom of the lake. I look forward and see a brilliant Light shining at the end of the tunnel.

Instantly, the freezing cold is gone; I feel warm. The horrible pain in my body is gone and I feel peaceful, calm, and very, very happy. The ringing in my ears and head is gone, replaced by a gentle silence, as if I were in the middle of a redwood forest with a gentle breeze blowing through the tops of the trees. The radiant Light, which looks like a thousand exploding suns, overtakes the blackness. My retinas should be burned out by its brightness, but I can stare into the Light and it doesn't hurt; it feels wonderful. Again,

◀ REMEMBERING THE LIGHT THROUGH PROSETRY*

I realize that all of the pain that consumed me an instant ago is completely gone. Warmth, joy, and an indescribable feeling of love replace the cold, terror, panic, and fear that enveloped me.

For some unknown reason, this dramatic rush toward the Light causes me no concern. I have no fear of the Light. I'm pulled closer and closer, as if I'm drawn into the Light by a giant, but gentle magnet.

Then, in the next instant, I'm suspended inside the center of an immense sphere, bigger than our high school gymnasium. The inside of the sphere looks like an enormous series of unending movie screens, with hundreds of movies playing in every direction, all at the same time. I am completely surrounded by images of my experiences. Wherever I look in the sphere, I see all the events of my lives; and I can hear, feel, touch, and smell the exact experience of living those lives. In this place there is no beginning; there is no end. I observe all of the moments of my lives all at the same time, all around me. My lifetimes are somehow mystically connected to each other. Strangely, I sense no fear or judgments, no guilt or accountability, and absolutely no blame or shame. I re-experience every thought, word, and action of each life experience whenever I focus on them. I am suspended in a world of unlimited dimensions.

After what seems like hours in the sphere, I am instantly back in the tunnel again, drawn toward the Light. I can actually feel its brightness, warmth, and love. As I get closer to the Light, I am absorbed by its brilliance and perfect love.

THE EVENT

I am in the Light! Oh my God, I am actually in the Light. I am the Light!

I look directly into the source of the Light and it appears to me in a human-like form. It looks like a massive, human silhouette radiating with the brightness of thousands of suns. Although I can't remember seeing its form before, somehow I recognize it. The Light speaks to me. *Andy, do not be afraid. Andy, I love you. Andy, we love you.*

The Light actually knows me. The Light knows my name. The Light called me Andy. Surrounding the central Light form are millions and millions of other Lights welcoming me back home. I know them all and they know me; we are all pieces of the same Light. I hear myself say, *It's good to be back home.* We are all together again.

Although I am in the Light, and the Light is in me, I am still Andy. I'm everywhere and I am in the Light at the same time. I see me as a person and I see me in the infinite, warm, and loving Light. I become the Light. The Light has a voice that I have never heard, yet it is not strange to me. The Light has a smile that is indescribably captivating and I recognize that too. The Light has an incredible sense of humor and an infectious laugh, and we talk and laugh together. The Light knows everything in the universe—and I don't have any questions, because I know everything that the Light knows, and that is everything!

The Light also knows every decision that I have ever made or will make, and the Light loves me without conditions. The Light loves me because of who I am—Andy, a piece of the

◄ REMEMBERING THE LIGHT THROUGH PROSETRY*

Light. There is no fear. No judgment. No punishment. No blame. No shame. No ledger of good and bad deeds. Only warmth, peace, joy, happiness, and love in the Light. I am one with the unconditionally loving Light.

I'm back home. I am home forever.

And then I am startled! The Light says, *Andy, you must go back.* And I say, *No, I'm not going back, I'm not leaving... I'm never, ever going back.* The Light says for a second time, *Andy, you must go back.* I repeat my first response. *No, I'm not going back...ever!* Just the thought of returning into my body back on earth is repulsive to me. I felt like I would be trying to force the universe into a tiny, brittle bottle. Then the Light says the third time, *Andy, you must go back.* The next instant, without pause or delay of the smallest increment of time, I am back on Earth...stuffed back into a cold, shivering, aching body lying on the beach. I open my eyes and tears roll down my cheeks. The Light is gone. Oh my God, the Light is gone! I am so sad, so mournful. I am back in this tired, achy, and nearly frozen body. How sad...how very, very sad I am. And I don't know why!

I am lying on my stomach on the sand. One of my friends pushes the rest of the water out of my lungs. I cough out the water, but the intense pain remains. This time the pain is different and permanent. It's the pain of being separated from the Light. I don't know why I'm so sad. I don't even know what I've just experienced. But I do know that all of the warmth, perfection, and love that was infused in my soul, I can no longer feel. The Light has played a devious trick on me. The Light allowed me to expand and become one with

THE EVENT

the Universe, and then rammed me back into my frail, earthly body. At the time, it seemed like a very cruel experience to put me through. I was very angry at the Light.

All my classmates stand around me, glad that I've been revived. Someone says, *Andy, you don't seem very happy about being dragged from the bottom of the lake. Are you still in a daze, or what? How was it? Were you afraid?* I answer with a lie. I say that I can't remember anything. I tell them that the entire episode is a complete blank. I have to lie to my friends, I have to lie to my family, and I have to lie to myself. I can't tell anyone about the Light. How can I expect them to understand what I just experienced if I don't understand any of it myself?

I tell myself that maybe it was just a hallucination or some bizarre connection of synapses inside my brain from the lack of oxygen, or something like that. I don't know. Maybe I'm just plain crazy. Oh well, I'll probably forget all about it in a little while.

It's been many, many years since my drowning and death, and I have forgotten thousands of experiences. Thousands of other experiences have faded and dimmed with the passing of time. Many traumatic memories have been embellished or partially forgotten. I have only one life and death experience that has remained clear and unchanged over my lifetime and this is it. The moment that I entered the Light, to become one with the Light, is a moment that has no other parallel in my life. It is a feeling of inexpressible, unconditional love, peace, and joy. It is a love that I cannot adequately describe with

REMEMBERING THE LIGHT THROUGH PROSETRY*

words; it's a love that can only be experienced. And I experienced it...I am in the Light, the Light is in me, and we are all One.

The poem that follows, "Death By Drowning and Back Again," describes my near death experience through the simple beauty of poetry written in the middle of the night.

THE EVENT

Death by Drowning and Back Again

Oh God, I'm drowning! My life is all black!
Why me? Why me, God? Please, can't I go back?
I sink into an abyss of ice-cold pain,
Surrounded by blackness again and again.
Though my senses are numb, my pain is intense
I scream out in silence—death seems so immense!

Every fiber of my body continues to fight
The ugly, frigid water is void of any light.
I continue to sink and struggle without end
Until finally, I hit bottom, alone without friend.
Stuck in the mud and try as I might
Escape is impossible from this black, hideous sight.

A voice from my depths tells me what's best.
"Let go, for just a moment, you need a little rest."
I'm afraid to stop trying for one breath of air
To rise from the bottom, break free from despair!
Again, the voice assures me, "Let go, it's all right
"After a brief moment, you can continue the fight."

All right then, okay then, I'll let go of my life
A moment of rest, and then on with my strife.
I release! I let go! Then in an instant so fine
I'm hurled from my body through a tunnel in time.
I look down and see my body all gnarled up in fright
I look up, and the tunnel is aglow in white Light.

⤺ REMEMBERING THE LIGHT THROUGH PROSETRY*

In a heartbeat, a gasp, my senses are alive.
I am warm, I am loved, I am happy—completely revived.
The Light is so bright it should burn through my eyes,
But it pulls like a gentle magnet, and then I realize
I'm engulfed in its brightness, with love and with care.
The Light, it sustains me…I can breathe its warm, sweet air.

And then in a moment I appear in a sphere.
My lives are all around me, I can see them, I can hear
Every moment, every thought through lifetimes unfolds.
There is no judgment or fear to behold,
No accounting, no damnation, just observations so clear
That my lives are just choices and it is love that endears.

"Don't be afraid," the Light says through my ears,
"I love you, we love you, and there's nothing to fear."
I'm welcomed by the Light—the Light smiles within me.
We talk, we play, we laugh, its love sets me free.
At last I am Home. The Universe is such a wondrous delight.
The Light is One in me…and I am One in the Light.

Surprisingly, the Light says, "You must go back."
"No, I'm finally Home!" I scream in a counterattack.
The Light insists, "Back to earth you must go."
Earthly images terrorize me and tears start to flow.
In an instant I am back, coughing up water on the sand
Earth's agony overshadows a Light so wonderfully grand.

CHAPTER 2

Remembering Eternity

IN THE LIGHT EVERYTHING WAS STRANGE, but at the same time, it was recognizable. I began to remember the exact details of everything as it burst into my awareness. I was conscious of the fact that nothing I was experiencing was totally new; all the experiences brought back familiar memories. It was like a homecoming after being away for a long, long time.

I never felt alienated. Even though I thought I was sensing all of the Light's attributes for the first time, somehow I was also remembering them. They were both unknown and familiar at the same time. The Light had a face I had never seen before, but yet, somehow I recognized it...I knew it. The Light had a voice I thought I had never heard before, but somehow I remembered it. The Light had a laugh and a smile that I encountered for the first time, but somehow I recalled it. Every attribute of the Light filled me with memories of love and joy! Every characteristic of the Light, and the countless billions of Lights surrounding it, immediately triggered remembrances. Therefore, even though in my mind, I thought I was in a place I had never been before, there was never a moment of fear or

◄ REMEMBERING THE LIGHT THROUGH PROSETRY*

apprehension. When I was in the Light, I was overwhelmed with the feeling that I was back home again—back where I knew I belonged. I still remember the words exactly as they cried out from my soul, "It's good to be back home."

I had been waking up in the middle of the night for a long time because of the many gnawing questions screaming at me from inside my mind. Why can't I adequately describe my experience in the Light? Why can't I put my emotional feelings down on paper so other people can know what I knew when I was immersed in the Light? What is my problem?

Then it came to me. I'm trying to do the impossible. I'm trying to describe an infinite Light using a finite toolbox. It's like trying to recreate the "Mona Lisa" on a piece of copy paper with a box of crayons. It's like trying to play Beethoven's Fifth Symphony with a piece of wax paper and a comb. Yes, I can do it, but I can't create the "soul" of the masterpiece because of inadequate tools.

Yes, I can attempt to describe my experience, my story, as a series of sequential events, but I can't find a way to describe the ecstasy and euphoria that consumed me. How do I describe being in eternity with crude, three-dimensional words? How do I describe my instantaneous transformation from a three-dimensional, thinking, and feeling being into the infinite-dimensional, all-knowing soul absorbed into the Light? Maybe the answer can be found in my attempt to describe the Light as it appeared to me in the middle of the night. Those nocturnal encounters always included an insistent and irresistible force compelling me to write poetry.

I thought of all the poetry that filled my head while I slept. Then, periodically, my streaming, subconscious thoughts would wake me up from a sound sleep...dancing and shouting at me from within my mind. I could see a poem written on a large, floating chalkboard. It was hanging there, waiting for me to copy it onto a piece of paper.

So, from time to time, in the peace and quiet of the early morning, I began to write down the poems that appeared to me in the silent space between my thoughts.

◄ REMEMBERING THE LIGHT THROUGH PROSETRY*

Being In The Light ... A Love Experience

Being in the Light ...
Is experiencing love without end.
Engulfed in warmth and kindness,
Cherished by an everlasting friend.

Being in the Light ...
Is releasing all sadness and pain.
Instantly, it's no longer important,
Peace is the overriding gain.

Being in the Light ...
Is passing from life through death.
Dying quickly or in agonizing pain,
Absorbed by love from Light's gentle breath.

Being in the Light ...
Is floating in a tunnel of darkness.
Seeing the bright Light of creation ahead,
Embraced by Light's love ever joyous.

Being in the Light ...
Is seeing life as simply choices.
Judged as neither good nor bad,
Acknowledged by heavenly voices.

Being in the Light ...
Is liberating for the timid and coy.
Discords of recent lifetimes,
Replaced with supernatural joy.

Being in the Light ...
Is realizing all life is worthy.
Being One with all the Universe,
Illuminated with celestial ecstasy.

Being in the Light ...
Is not limited by dimensions three.
Being everywhere at the speed of thought,
Body, mind, and soul completely free.

Being in the Light ...
Is floating in the center of eternity.
Yesterday, today, and tomorrow,
Interwoven in perfection and clarity.

Being in the Light ...
Is transcending all space and time.
Being a piece of the Infinite Light,
Immersed unconditionally in a Cosmos sublime.

CHAPTER 3

Early Childhood Visions

RELIGION WAS THE CENTRAL FOCUS of my extended family. I learned to fear God and make sure I didn't stray from his teachings. My parents taught me their version of reality, and the differences between right and wrong. If I did anything wrong, the consequences would be disastrous; I would go directly to Hell and stay there for all eternity. And that's a long time.

These fear-based, core beliefs permeated all my thoughts, decisions, and actions as a maturing child. I tried to be a "good boy" and spent much of my time reading religious books, praying, and attending countless religious services. My religious beliefs were the fundamental elements in forming my personality and social interactions. I turned into a frightened pleaser. I always tried to please my parents, my relatives, my teachers...everyone. The result of all of this fear-based, pleasing lifestyle is that I grew into a very timid, introverted, and fearful person.

One of the main disturbing concepts I learned was separation. I was taught we were better than everyone else because

◄ REMEMBERING THE LIGHT THROUGH PROSETRY*

we belonged to God's church and were following His truth. Other people, who didn't believe in our God, wouldn't be saved. They would perish in everlasting fire. We were better than all of the others and should never get too close to any of them.

In contrast, even as a child, I personally felt a "oneness" with everyone and everything around me. I tried to explain the oneness I felt to my parents by describing some of the many visions and images I had about living in a different world. It was a world aglow in a loving white light! This was a place where everyone was different, but we loved each other and celebrated our differences with patience and understanding. But every time I tried to explain this to my parents and relatives I was ridiculed and told that these daydreams were probably thoughts from the devil. So finally, I decided never to share these visions with anyone again and forced myself to forget them.

It took a Near Death Experience to reopen the story of my life's journey by awakening my original, suppressed, personal core beliefs. It took many more years for me to replace my fear-based beliefs with love-based ones. But, the journey was truly worth the effort and the energy.

Years after my NDE, I began to understand the oneness I always felt as a child actually came from memories I experienced in previous lifetimes. It is what I, unconsciously, must have been searching for and trying to remember in my early childhood years.

I have spent years trying to find a way to describe the

visions that I had as a child. Finally, a few years ago, these visions came back to me again.

They always came to me in the middle of the night—visions wrapped in words—words spiraling around in my head, over and over again. They didn't stop spinning until I wrote them down. And this time they came out of my mind as a poem I call "Childhood Visions."

◄ REMEMBERING THE LIGHT THROUGH PROSETRY*

Childhood Visions

When I was a child I had visions of a land
That was aglow in white light, wherever you stand.
We laughed, we played; we were safe all day long.
We delighted in each other, singing life's sweet song.
We were all one—no killing, fear, or hate.
We were all one—what a wondrous, glorious state!

When I was a child I had visions of a place
That was filled with people of every color, belief, and race.
We celebrated our differences, what made us unique.
Each person was important, everyone got to speak.
We were all one—we stood together, hand in hand.
We were all one—true peace was alive in our land.

When I was a child I shared my visions and my world.
The self-righteous condemned me, insults were hurled.
"Others are the wrong color, wrong religion, wrong sex!
God made us special, it's written in His holy text.
We are God's chosen—we're saved by the bell.
We are God's chosen—all the others are going to Hell!"

Now I remember, I know it's life's great start,
Visions from my childhood are real and alive in my heart.
As a rainbow's brilliant colors come from white light above
We can replace terror, hatred, and fear with our love.
We are all one—the idea is beautiful and true.
We are all one—it's simple and easy to do.

Now we have visions of our planet from the sky.
Now our visions no longer harbor lies.
We can see that war isn't an answer, peace is a choice.
Life is wonderful when we speak with one voice.
We are all one—no one way is the best.
We are all one—it's life's ultimate test.

CHAPTER 4

Breathing In The Present Moment

I WAS ALIVE, suspended in the center of a colossal, sphere-like theater. It was like being inside of a gigantic basketball the size of a convention hall. I was completely surrounded by countless screens everywhere I looked: up, down, front, back, left, and right. Displayed on these screens were all of my lives, both here on Earth and on other worlds. I felt, tasted, smelled, and heard each experience. As I viewed them, I relived each and every event exactly as I remembered it when it occurred. Everywhere I looked there was a life experience connected to another life experience, connected to another life experience...seamlessly etched on the gigantic screen through invisible and undetectable connections.

I saw myself as a baby, a young man, a woman, an old person, and with all of the people I met in my many life journeys. I relived the joys of past friendships, good works, and loves. I viewed and experienced the pain and suffering that also was occurring. I could see and recall the feelings of all those I interacted with throughout time in their present moment.

◄ REMEMBERING THE LIGHT THROUGH PROSETRY*

Although everything was happening at once, I experienced each specific event that I focused on in the time frame in which it occurred. Deep within me, I knew that I was in what I now call the Eternal Now.

In the sphere of the Eternal Now I experienced all the events both sequentially and simultaneously. This reality is beyond all earthly, three-dimensional explanations. In the Eternal Now everything occurs concurrently, both sequentially and simultaneously. I relived each of my lives individually and sequentially; but in the same moment I simultaneously relived all of my other lives too. I understood and comprehended each permutation of my existence completely. I realized that the Eternal Now exists in every moment—in other words, the only moment that really exists is the moment of Now.

A few years ago I kept waking up in the middle of the night with a phrase going around and around in my head, "The moment is now, the moment is now." It wouldn't stop, so I got up and started to meditate. In the middle of my meditation I knew that I had to start writing down the images and words that were whirling around in my mind. I got a pencil and pad of paper and I stared at the blank sheet before me. In the still, early morning I could hear my breathing, slow and deep, as I started to write.

(What follows are the thoughts that went through my mind as I was writing each verse. After the last verse I have included the poem in its entirety.)

BREATHING IN THE PRESENT MOMENT

It's amazing how wonderful just one breath of air can be! When I was drowning in the ice-cold muck at the bottom of the lake, I would have given anything for just one breath of air. My body was in such agonizing pain; every cell in my body was crying out for oxygen. It was unbearable! Then finally, with no other options available to me, I let go of my hold on life. I just quit struggling and let go.

Letting go instantly freed me from all my pain, fear, and suffering. I was able to breathe again. Letting go released my despair! Freezing cold turned into warmth. Excruciating pain turned into joy and pleasure. The deafening screeching noise in my ears turned into the serenity of silence. The frightening darkness at the bottom of the lake turned into a bright, intense Light. Fear turned into love. And all of these transitions occurred instantaneously.

Letting go was the answer to my pain in the bottom of the lake years ago…and letting go is the answer to my pain today. Letting go in the moment of now.

As I listen to my breath …
To the sweet sound of air,
Breathing in fills me with hope,
Breathing out releases my despair.

I have a real appreciation for breathing. I love to breathe. It's exhilarating for me, especially when I remember that I couldn't breathe for what seemed like an eternity. And every breath centers me into the "now" of the moment

◄ REMEMBERING THE LIGHT THROUGH PROSETRY*

I am experiencing. Many times during the day I tell myself that the moment is now! Right now! Not tomorrow, next week, or next year—but now!

I stop myself from thinking. I focus all of my energy on taking the next deep breath...in and out...and I fully concentrate on the moment. I can feel myself filling with Light. It's astounding this moment of now. It brings everything into perspective for me. It is part of my promise to myself—to pay attention to my breathing and the moment of now.

A beautiful rhythm,
As my breaths rise and fall.
Dissolving the discords of life
Into moments of now.

The *now* fills me with freedom. It releases me from the illusions of life here in my three-dimensional world. There is something that is truly "freeing" for me in the moment of now. When I stop what I am *doing* to *be* in the moment, I am filled with a Light that is freeing and loving. Freedom and love! Those two words go together, and are interchangeable. Being filled with the Light of love fills me with freedom too. Yesterday is gone and tomorrow may not come, but I do have this moment of now, and that is where I choose to live. And every time that I choose to live in the moment of now—I choose to live in freedom!

The moment is now ...
What a powerful thought.

BREATHING IN THE PRESENT MOMENT

*It's wrapped in a freedom
That can't be sold or bought.*

As I am breathing in the now, I can feel a smile forming on my face. I can't help but smile. The smile comes from within; it comes from within the Light. I smile because I know that with each breath I am being filled with an unconditional love, and that love goes directly into my heart. I realize that my burdens are just illusions and images; my true reality is the reality I choose in the present moment.

*The moment is now ...
Brings a smile to my face.
As the images that burden my heart
Are infused with a loving grace.*

All the traumas of my life melt away and are replaced with an inner calm and beauty, and are enhanced with every breath. In the moment of now, I can see that all the traumas of my life are illusions—they are there because I have put them there. I know I am creating my own reality and I can create it with trauma or calm and beauty. The choice is always mine. I can change my reality whenever I choose; all it takes is a return to an awareness of my breathing.

*The moment is now ...
Refocuses my life.*

◄ REMEMBERING THE LIGHT THROUGH PROSETRY*

Calm and beauty replace
Illusions of trauma and strife.

Reviewing my lives in the sphere, I perceived no feelings of judgment, guilt, blame, or shame in any event, only unconditional acceptance. My conversations with the Light opened my heart and it became apparent that, for me, there are no right or wrong actions. I saw that all my actions were mere choices that either worked or didn't work for me, and for those around me. The Light did not judge my choices as right or wrong. The Light did not condemn, humiliate, punish, or rebuke me…no, not at all, the Light just loved me. The Light loved me for being me, and for being a piece of the Light.

The moment is now …
No more guilt, blame, or shame,
No judgment or separation
In the Light we are all the same.

When I drowned and was absorbed by the Light, I instantly experienced what true unconditional love is. The Light welcomed me into itself, spoke to me, and said: "Andy, do not be afraid," "Andy, I love you," and "Andy, we love you." I was immediately overwhelmed by the Light's unconditional love. I was aware of the Light's love flowing through me into the existing Universe. In addition to being loved, I actually "became" the love in the Light.

BREATHING IN THE PRESENT MOMENT

The moment is now ...
Gathering forces waiting to be,
Imbue love into Being
Radiating unconditionally through me.

As I am writing these words, I am transformed back into the Light. Even after all these years—I feel as if I am in the Light right now.

When I am in the Light, I find that I am vibrating in unison with the Light, completely absorbed by the Light, and I am One with the Light—but at the same time I am still Andy. My individual nature is retained in the exact moment that it is melted, absorbed, and fused into the Light. It is a glorious contradiction of experiences—a wondrous feeling of being an individual and yet, vibrating as One with the whole Universe.

The moment is now ...
My life is joyful and fun.
The moment is now ...
In the Light we're all vibrating as One.

◄ REMEMBERING THE LIGHT THROUGH PROSETRY*

The Moment Is Now

As I listen to my breath,
To the sweet sound of air,
Breathing in fills me with hope,
Breathing out releases my despair.

A beautiful rhythm,
As my breaths rise and fall.
Dissolving the discords of life
Into moments of now.

The moment is now ...
What a powerful thought.
It's wrapped in a freedom
That can't be sold or bought.

The moment is now ...
Brings a smile to my face.
As images that burden my heart
Are infused with a loving grace.

The moment is now ...
Refocuses my life.
Calm and beauty replace
Illusions of trauma and strife.

The moment is now ...
No more guilt, blame, or shame,
No judgment or separation
In the Light we are all the same.

BREATHING IN THE PRESENT MOMENT

The moment is now ...
Gathering forces waiting to be,
Imbue love into Being
Radiating unconditionally through me.

The moment is now ...
My life is joyful and fun.
The moment is now ...
In the Light we're all vibrating as One.

CHAPTER 5

We Are All Pieces Of The Light

I REMEMBERED BEING IN THE LIGHT after I had drowned. I remembered exchanging thoughts with the Light. The Light revealed how people on earth have been killing each other in the name of God since the beginning of our history. The Light continued to reveal that the reason for these hateful acts is our basic belief in fear and separation. Fear and separation enable and encourage our mutual suicidal destruction. The Light told me that when we realize we are all One, all pieces of the same holographic Light, then our wars and killing will stop. Hatred and destruction will be replaced with peace and love. It will no longer make any sense to kill each other, because we will all realize that when we hate and kill someone else, we are actually hating and killing ourselves too. We will finally remember and understand the meaning of true humanity—we are all vibrating as One because we are all One.

During the night, after the 9/11 terrorist attack, I couldn't sleep. Obviously, my physical world had changed and I felt an uncontrolled anger building up inside of me. I was filled with

◀ REMEMBERING THE LIGHT THROUGH PROSETRY*

anger toward the terrorists who wanted to destroy our world; and that they were doing it in the name of God angered me even more. How dumb and mindless, I thought. How could they do an evil act like that in God's name?

Since I couldn't sleep I decided to meditate. During my meditation I could see a bright blue light in my mind's eye. There were two phrases coming out of the blue light, repeating over and over again, "Pieces of God!" and "Pieces of the Light!"

Pieces of God! Pieces of the Light! I never heard those phrases before. How could God be in pieces? What did it mean? It sounded like an oxymoron. It sounded strange and obtuse.

Weeks went by, and every time I meditated those six words would automatically appear in my meditation. It was very disturbing to me.

Then, one night, I finally understood what "Pieces of God" and "Pieces of the Light" meant to me personally. I immediately felt the urge to write. So, I got up and started writing the thoughts that flooded quickly through my mind. After an hour I was finished. I was very tired and went back to sleep. When I got up in the morning I picked up the pad and read what I wrote a few hours earlier. It was titled "Pieces of God ... Pieces of Light."

WE ARE ALL PIECES OF THE LIGHT

Pieces of God ... Pieces of Light

Pieces of God abide all around us,
Pieces of God in the air, land, and sea,
Pieces of God in the oceans and mountains...
Pieces of Light are inside you and me.

Pieces of God in the hot, humid summer,
Pieces of God in the warm spring and cool fall,
Pieces of God in the death of the winter...
Pieces of Light in the seasons of us all.

Pieces of God in the bombs in Jerusalem,
Pieces of God in the terror of Iran,
Pieces of God walking the streets of South Chicago...
Pieces of Light in every child, woman, and man.

Pieces of God in the hurricanes in New Orleans,
Pieces of God in the earthquakes of LA,
Pieces of God in the flooded Mississippi...
Pieces of Light by the thousands help and pray.

Pieces of God in the killing fields of Asia,
Pieces of God in the suicide bombs of Iraq,
Pieces of God in the hatred from terrorists...
Pieces of Light going all the way back.

Pieces of God come in every shape, size, and color,
Pieces of God exist in every mind, soul, and heart,
Pieces of God abide in our universe, sun, and planet...
Pieces of Light embedded in us all from the start.

◀ **REMEMBERING THE LIGHT THROUGH PROSETRY***

I see Pieces of God in the smile of a baby,
I see Pieces of God in an old, wrinkled face,
I see Pieces of God in our death and re-birth cycles…
I'm overjoyed as all the Pieces of Light fall into place.

CHAPTER 6

Vibrations Remembered

WHEN I LEFT MY BODY at the bottom of the lake, my soul was instantaneously transformed by a pulsating energy. This energy was vibrating at a frequency that infused me with unimaginable feelings of love, contentment, and ecstasy.

Everything that surrounded me was vibrating. The vibrations formed millions of fantastic, pulsating colors. It was as if I were dipped into an endless sea of rainbows, each one more colorful and beautiful than the previous. Especially white...I could have never imagined the countless variations of white. The hues and shades of white mesmerized me for what seemed like an eternity. The totality of energy was vibrating through an infinite number of frequencies. Each frequency created yet another aspect of the Universe. From the smallest vibrating string of creation to the largest super galaxy—they were all vibrating in their own colorful sources.

Each vibration had a part to play in the creation of the Universe, and I remembered my many roles in this cosmic symphony. I could observe myself playing out the assorted illusions

REMEMBERING THE LIGHT THROUGH PROSETRY*

in my many incarnations. They were all occurring in the universal moment of now; but there was no confusion on my part, since I could understand each and every one of them concurrently. Then, for an instant, I watched myself choose love over fear. I could actually see the surrounding vibrations increase their frequencies and harmonies as the love decision blossomed.

I kept waking up in the middle of the night for weeks with the word "vibrations" tumbling around in my mind. Vibrations, vibrations, it wouldn't stop. What was it supposed to mean to me—especially in the middle of the night? I'd think about it for a while, and then go back to sleep—only to wake up the next night with the same word dancing around in my mind.

Then, one night the word started to take on a familiar form. It began to look like an image of me as I was leaving my body at the bottom of the lake, vibrating and floating through the tunnel toward the Light. I was vibrating in the tunnel with an energy that gave me an overwhelming sensation of being completely and unconditionally loved. It was a very personal, vibrating energy—it was my energy, but at the same time I knew it was the energy of everything else that exists.

Suddenly, I found myself holding a pen and writing on a pad of paper. I was writing a poem—a poem titled "Vibrations." As soon as I finished writing I became very tired and went back to sleep. When I woke in the morning I picked up the pad and read what I had written just a few hours earlier. As I read the poem I could actually feel the vibrations that were surrounding me, and in me, when I was absorbed by the Light on the other side.

VIBRATIONS REMEMBERED

Vibrations

Vibrations abide in the heart and soul of all
Energy lives in everything, large and small.

Vibrating strings create existence from none
Awaken and alive until their frequency is gone.

Harmony fuses all experiences into lifetimes
Atoms to galaxies, the simple to the sublime.

Lower frequencies create linear time and mass
Higher ones release the now from future and past.

Frequencies of separation, fear, and hatred are low
Stagnating in still, lifeless, dark pools of the ego.

The higher the oscillations the brighter the Light
Loving, caring, and oneness—illuminating sights.

Unconditional love vibrates throughout the soul
Its frequency heals, making shattered lives whole.

Unconditional acceptance resonates equally as high
Releasing the shackles of fear, to soar through the sky.

Holographic Universes pulsate in parallel realms
Comprehending through an earthly mind overwhelms.

Infinite pieces of Light shine like billions of suns
Vibrating as individuals, yet all fusing into One.

CHAPTER 7

What Is Unconditional Love?

NOT ONLY WAS THE LOVE I FELT IN THE LIGHT unconditional and nonjudgmental, but it was also very personal. The Light's love was directed into me, embedded in me, and manifested itself as an unconditional acceptance of myself. I lost any sense of right and wrong or of good and bad. The recollections of my earthly life just contained actions and events. Some of my actions filled me with joy and others with sorrow, but none of my actions was ever judged—either by me or by the Light.

At the moment of my earth-death, when I let go, I was not aware that I was dead. I was aware of the fact that I wasn't in my body anymore, since I saw it stuck in the mud at the bottom of the lake. But I wasn't "disoriented," to the contrary; I was elated because I immediately felt warm, safe, and loved. I couldn't understand until I remembered that I was ecstatic because the "terror" of the previous instant was gone. It was as if the excruciating pain I had just endured never really happened to me. It felt as if it happened to someone else, like I was just an observer.

◀ REMEMBERING THE LIGHT THROUGH PROSETRY*

It was another middle of the night awakening in which I encountered a phrase spinning around in my mind, and it wouldn't let me go back to sleep. So, I got up and sat down at my desk and allowed the phrase to develop.

"Unconditional Love." An interesting phrase, but what did it really mean to me? I didn't know the answer immediately, so I started to write down the feelings that were whirling around on the chalkboard in my mind. As I was writing, I became aware of a feeling of love so overwhelming, so overpowering, it had no equal here on earth. The "oneness" I felt with every atom in the Universe fused me into a state of eternal bliss—yet, I still retained my individual self-awareness. Concepts and behaviors like judgment, separation, superiority, and condemnation appeared as shallow, lifeless, decaying actions that sucked the life out of the world. What a waste of thought and energy!

I remembered that my encounters in the Light revolved around choices. All I had to do was choose to love, choose to accept, and choose to see the oneness that resides in the eyes and hearts of each of us…to experience unconditional love.

I finished the short poem and went back to sleep. The next morning I read "Unconditional Love" and felt the same breathtaking, all-encompassing, unconditional love that I experienced when I penned it.

WHAT IS UNCONDITIONAL LOVE?

Unconditional Love

When I choose to love unconditionally
And I choose to accept unconditionally
I experience unconditional love.

When I replace judgment with observation
And condemnation with acceptance
I experience unconditional love.

When I stop blaming and shaming
And embrace our shared experiences
I experience unconditional love.

When I relinquish my superiority
And cease ridiculing your inferiority
I experience unconditional love.

When I highlight our Oneness
And celebrate our differences
I experience unconditional love.

When I reject our separation
And promote our collective Oneness
I experience unconditional love.

When I see my eyes in your eyes
And feel all our hearts beating as One
I experience unconditional love.

When I choose to love unconditionally
And I choose to accept unconditionally
I am unconditional love.

CHAPTER 8

Why Not Try Love?

AFTER THE 9/11 ATTACKS on the World Trade Towers, I awoke from a sound sleep realizing that after all of the terrible events I have experienced in my lifetime, nothing has really changed in the world. I lay in bed thinking about what I had witnessed through my lifetime.

My earliest childhood memories are of World War II and the overwhelming fear that we were going to be overrun by our enemies. As a child I had recurring nightmares about being caught and killed by the enemy. Finally, the war was over and it looked like there would be peace forever.

Not so. Next came the communist bloc, the Korean War, and the Vietnam War. At last, after almost 50 years of the Cold War the "walls came tumbling down," most of the communist bloc dissolved, and true peace would reign on earth in my lifetime.

Not so again! Next I got to experience worldwide terrorism. It seemed to me, the more advanced we became from a technological point of view, the more insidious the fear and disorder became which prevailed throughout the world.

So, there I lay, my mind churning up images of my lifetime spent in a fear-and-separation-based world. After all of the social, economic, and humanitarian attempts at world peace—nothing really worked. It seems like the only thing, collectively, we didn't try was love and acceptance. Why not try that? What do we have to lose? The world couldn't get any worse than it is at the present time.

I got out of bed and began to write a poem about those confusing thoughts that were spinning around in my mind. The next morning I read what I had written. It is a poem titled "Give Love A Chance."

Give Love A Chance

Life is full of infinite choices.
Life is full of varied voices.
Life is full of love and fear.
While bombs are dropping far and near,
Why are we stumbling in this Hellish dance?
Why not choose Love? Give Love a chance.

Life is paved with divergent roads.
Different people carry different loads.
Our days and nights are filled with dreams,
But we're awakened by our horrible screams,
Killing each other in God's name enhanced.
Why not choose Love instead? Give Love a chance.

Life is filled with countless feelings.
Some cause hate; some cause healings.
When our lives are lived in hate,
We stop feeling Love. We only berate.
Those who don't believe as we—are killed by hateful glances!
Why not choose Love? Life says, give Love some chances.

Life is wrapped in endless joy.
It's ours to nurture or destroy.
Life is present in our every breath.
We are all One—in both life and death,
So let's all embrace in a peaceful dance.
Why choose Love? Because Love's our last chance!

CHAPTER 9

Creating Random Acts Of Joy

EVER SINCE I CAME BACK FROM THE LIGHT, I have had the experience of being filled with a feeling of complete joy. I am overwhelmed with joy for no apparent reason. The sensation of pure joy puts a smile on my face that I can't remove. It is a wonderful feeling of contentment and happiness that has no obvious internal or external source. The amount of time that this joyous feeling consumes me varies from a few minutes to days.

These random feelings of joy bring all of my observations and actions into perspective. The ever-present feelings of drama that normally accompany my daily activities are gone—replaced by a truer perspective, which puts events into their proper place in my life. Gone are the tension, anxiety, and fear that surround my normal activities; they are replaced with a calm and loving acceptance. During these moments of joy I view my daily activities and associations as opportunities to respond with unconditional love and acceptance. I even view the most trying situations I face as opportunities to respond with love and kindness.

◄ REMEMBERING THE LIGHT THROUGH PROSETRY*

Soon I began to experience overwhelming feelings of joy as a result of initiating loving actions on my part first. I am able to reverse the unexpected joyful process. Instead of waiting for this random feeling of joy to engulf me, I can initiate the feeling by creating random acts of caring first. And during these acts of caring, I sense an overwhelming feeling of joy that absorbs and illuminates me.

A few weeks after I first experienced this joyful revelation, a wonderful dream woke me up in the middle of the night. As soon as I was awake I felt a gentle force pulling me out of bed and urging me to write about these random acts of joy that were in my dream. So, very quietly, I found my pen and paper and started to write "Random Acts Of Joy."

Random Acts Of Joy

Waking up in the middle of the night
Thoughts spinning around, forcing me to write.

Listening to those who cry out in pain
Truly listening, no thought of personal gain.
A random act of joy.

Remembering injustices from the past
Forgiving all wrongdoers at last.
A random act of joy.

Observing hatred and judgment on earth
Releasing Light's vibration for a loving rebirth.
A random act of joy.

Accepting everyone the world despises
Seeing the love from the Light in their eyes
A random act of joy.

Assuring children they're all worthwhile
Wiping their tears, exchanging smiles.
A random act of joy.

Embracing those who have lost it all
Sharing my fortunes when the needy call.
A random act of joy.

Keeping a warm, loving smile on my face
Giving those I meet a calm, caring grace.
A random act of joy.

◄ REMEMBERING THE LIGHT THROUGH PROSETRY*

Rejecting separation, guilt, blame, and shame
Vibrating in the Light, we're all the same.
A random act of joy.

Waking up in the middle of the night
A heart filled with love to make the world right.

CHAPTER **10**

Who Is A True Friend?

THEN IT HAPPENED. After over 40 years I had the phone number of one of my best high school and college friends. It took years of intermittent work on the Internet, but I was finally successful. I had his number.

I was very eager to talk to him again after all these years. We had been so close through high school and the early college years. It would be so good to get back together again and share our life stories. I dialed his number and waited with anticipation for his phone to be picked up. "Hello, this is an old friend from your past, Andy Petro. How have you been, Bob?" A long pause and then, "How did you find my number?" What? After all these years, his first comment to me is "How did you find my number?"

We exchanged small talk for a few minutes. Then he said he had a client coming into his office and he couldn't talk anymore. He continued saying if I gave him my number he would call back after his appointment. He never did.

◄ REMEMBERING THE LIGHT THROUGH PROSETRY*

A few months after my discovery call, I woke up in the middle of the night. My mind was spinning with the phrase "a true friend." What did that phrase really mean to me? And why wouldn't it go away? So I got up and started writing.

The following morning I read what I had written. My disappointment in my previous conversation with Bob had vanished. I remembered what true friendship is really about and where to find it.

A True Friend

*I have searched the world from end to end.
I have looked in every corner, around every bend.
And of all the gifts that God ever did send,
The most precious is a true and trusting friend.*

*A true friend is as rare as a diamond.
A true friend is more priceless than gold.
A true friend always supports you,
When the world thinks you're useless and old.*

*A true friend is a kindred spirit,
Who is there in the dark of the night.
Who holds your hand and comforts you,
As you journey back into the Light.*

*A true friend lasts more than a lifetime,
Whether in minutes, in days or in years.
A true friend is always by your side,
To support you, and help calm your fears.*

*A true friend is disguised as a neighbor,
A mother, a brother, a man on the street.
A true friend goes back to your childhood,
And is hiding in the next person you meet.*

CHAPTER 11

How Many Choices?

IN MY LIFE REVIEW I PERCEIVED no feelings of judgment, guilt, blame, or shame in any event I experienced—only unconditional acceptance. My conversations with the Light opened my heart and I became aware that there are no right or wrong actions—merely choices. All my actions are choices that either worked or didn't work for me and those around me. When my actions worked, they were choices that fostered love and joy; when they didn't work, they created fear and pain. Many choices kept me down and feeling like a victim, while others elevated me to feelings of peace and joy. My life was a continuous stream of personal choices.

ᕤᕤᕤᕤᕤᕤ

It was a hot summer night. I woke up covered in sweat. The dream I had was lucid. I could still feel its effects as I lay there awake. My dream was about the countless choices I have made during my lifetime. And in my dream, I was back in the sphere with the Light reviewing my life's choices again. I was observing the choices I was continually making and

REMEMBERING THE LIGHT THROUGH PROSETRY*

noticing how they affected my perception of being alive and the people who interacted with me.

I could see all the possibilities in each and every choice I made. My life had many directions and possibilities; and I could view and understand all of the different paths that were created by the decisions I made and those I didn't make. It was like the branches of a giant oak tree growing out into the Universe, and the unique path that I took in this incarnation was a glowing, golden passageway to the top of the tree.

The phrase "three choices" kept spinning around in my mind. Over and over again, three choices. I knew it was going to be another of my sleepless nights unless I got up to write about my choices. I went into the den and began to write.

HOW MANY CHOICES?

Three Choices

I woke up in the middle of the night
Filled with fear, foreboding, and fright.
My body was covered in sweat and pain
I knew I was making choices again and again.

I remembered the measure of the depth of my fear
Depends on my choices, the illusions I hold dear.
I am a piece of the Light, I am One with All
I create my realities from thoughts big and small.

Thoughts are creations that exist within me.
A single thought can enslave or set me free.
My thoughts aren't judged as good or bad,
They're only manifested as joyful or sad.

Thoughts I create abide in my world.
Embedded as choices, waiting to be unfurled.
The first one views life with dread,
Give up! Cry out! Choose to be a victim instead!

The second one is available from the Light above.
It changes perceptions from fear to love.
No one pulls my strings; choices are always mine,
My perceptions are my creations each and every time.

The third choice is a wonderful, powerful tool.
It enables me to recreate reality anew.
I choose thoughts that fill me with joy and delight
Of an unconditional, loving Universe aglow in white Light.

CHAPTER **12**

Touch—An Awesome Dream

I WOKE UP IN THE MIDDLE OF AN AWESOME DREAM. I was dreaming I was in another space-time universe. I was surrounded by and infused with a loving and peaceful Light. Even though I was awake, the mental images from my dream were as clear as if I were still dreaming. I was able to relive all of the details of the dream while I was lying in bed awake.

In my dream, my sense of touch was increased a million fold. When I touched a rose petal I not only felt the coolness and smoothness of the flower on my fingertips, but I felt it within my whole being. It was as if I became the rose. I knew what it felt like to "be a rose." In my dream I found myself walking on a beach with the surf breaking at my feet. I felt each and every grain of sand under my feet. I sensed the oneness of each piece of sand, and how it was a reflection of the entire universe. I could feel the surf lapping around and touching my feet and instantly I became one with the ocean in all its majesty and glory. When I looked up at the sky I saw every single star as unique in its own essence, but combining with all the other stars composing the totality of the infinite cosmos.

◄ REMEMBERING THE LIGHT THROUGH PROSETRY*

These feelings were so overpowering I couldn't move. Then, finally, as if by magic, I found myself standing beside my bed and I began walking toward the den. I picked up a pen and a pad of paper, sat down, and started to write about the wonders of touch—both here on earth and in the unending universe of the Light.

The next morning I went back into the den and read what I had written a few hours before...it was simply called "Touch."

Touch

*Touch is a perfect gift from the Light
Transforming fingers into sound, smell and sight.*

*Touch a baby's smooth and gentle skin
Feel its soul smile, the Universe spin.*

*Touch your love's lips and cheek
Become one without having to speak.*

*Touch an old wrinkled hand
Relive a long lifetime, begin to understand.*

*Touch a homeless stranger passing by
Share dignity and oneness in each other's eyes.*

*Touch the rain as it falls upon an uplifted face
Enjoy being cleansed by heaven's loving grace.*

*Touch a fresh rose petal wet with dew
Smell the beauty of creation there too.*

*Touch a redwood reaching tall into the sky
Hear the hush of a cathedral as the wind passes by.*

*Touch ocean waves lapping at your feet
Visit the birthplace of all earthly life we meet.*

*Touch the solitude engulfing a foggy shore
Listen to the ocean, hear the seagulls soar.*

◄ REMEMBERING THE LIGHT THROUGH PROSETRY*

Touch the wonder of a gentle, sunny day
Absorb the energy from its solar spray.

Touch the sky with a curious, searching reach
Comprehend the infinite in the absence of speech.

Touch the Light emanating from the sun
Igniting all humanity and life into One.

CHAPTER 13

What Does It Mean To Be Human?

WHY AM I A HUMAN BEING? I have often wondered, what does being human really mean to me?

One night I had a marvelous dream in which I could see, feel, and experience my life from its first moments on planet earth. I saw my life through both the bright lens of love and the dark lens of fear. My life was filled with contradictions. It wasn't that I wasn't loved, but the love I experienced was always conditional. And fear was always at the core of the conditions.

My dream produced visions of myself as I evolved from a tiny baby through to old age. My early life was always filled with questions relative to the pain and misery that we forced on each other. Why was I taught separation as a child? Why was it the basic tenet of my early life? Why did I live my early life believing in separation when I knew, in my heart of hearts, it was just an illusion? I knew, down deep in my soul, we all are pieces of the same Light.

REMEMBERING THE LIGHT THROUGH PROSETRY*

I lay there with thoughts of what all of this meant to me—to be in this human form. What does it really mean to be human? I couldn't shift those thoughts from my mind and return to sleep. I felt driven to write "To Be Human."

WHAT DOES IT MEAN TO BE HUMAN?

To Be Human

What does it mean to be human?
To fall from the stars to this place
To come from love everlasting
And walk this planet without grace?

What does it mean to be fearful?
To be pushed from the warmth of the womb
To be yanked, slapped, cold and crying
Terrorized by the light of this new tomb?

What does it mean to be helpless?
To be tiny—unable to communicate
To be at the mercy of giants
Trying to understand life in this state?

What does it mean to learn separation?
To exchange love for bigotry and fear
To sense the loss of eternal Oneness
As suspicion, anger, and hatred appear?

What does it mean to be three-dimensional?
To be locked in a finite time and space
Unable to move at the speed of thought
Confined to the relative all over the place?

What does it mean to experience emotions?
To be happy, sad, in love or in hate
To encounter the full range of feelings
Trapped in a body, trying to relate?

❧ REMEMBERING THE LIGHT THROUGH PROSETRY*

What does it mean to be human?
It's accepting the gift of free choice
It's remembering the Light of Oneness
Choosing to love, accept, and rejoice!

CHAPTER 14

Cancer And The Light

IT SEEMED LIKE A NORMAL DOCTOR'S OFFICE VISIT. I had a fever and infection and made an appointment to pick up a prescription to stop my coughing. I had forgotten that I had taken a series of tests for my annual physical a couple of weeks before. When I got to the office I was told that the doctor wanted to see me. He surprised me by telling me that one of the tests came back, and by the way, I had cancer.

I was shocked! What? I had cancer? Impossible! I was in perfect health, and cancer would never happen to me!

I became very angry and depressed. How could this happen to me? Over and over again, cancer was all that I was thinking about. It went on for days.

And then one night I woke up a little after midnight with the phrase "a love poem to cancer" spinning around in my mind. That was a strange phrase. It was so intense that the only way to alleviate the feeling was to leave my bed and write the words that were flowing through my heart and mind.

REMEMBERING THE LIGHT THROUGH PROSETRY*

I awoke the next morning and read what I had written. By the time I finished reading the poem I remembered being in the Light—my anger, depression, and self-pity vanished—I was calm and filled with peace. I decided to make my cancer experience a source of rebirth and love, both for me and for all those around me.

(A year later I was healed by the Light...and some innovative technologies.)

CANCER AND THE LIGHT

A Love Poem To Cancer

I woke up at three o'clock in the morning
Filled with self-pity and forlorning.
The news was still fresh—only a few days old.
I saw the doctor's face, detached and cold.

My fever was the reason for the short office stay.
It had been with me for more than a day.
He said, "Take some of this." I squirmed where I sat.
I was ready to go home, it seemed as quick as that.

"Oh, by the way, your biopsy came back yesterday.
The results aren't very good, I'm afraid to say.
I know you won't like the lab's answer,
But many of your cells mutated to cancer!"

What did I hear as the words bounced off the wall?
Was he talking about me? My biopsy and all?
No! It couldn't be me! There must be a mistake?
It was like being ripped open with a flaming hot rake!

Am I not One in the Light? How can this be?
A disease like this could never happen to me!
I was outraged, disillusioned, I lost my breath!
I felt abandoned—I was overcome by death.

Why me? Why me? It seemed so unfair.
Why me? I screamed into the hot afternoon air.
Then the Light touched me, I could see it and hear
The Light is within me. Its Love replaced my fear.

◄ REMEMBERING THE LIGHT THROUGH PROSETRY*

The cancer is in me, it's been here awhile.
But now I can live with Love and a smile.
I'll let unconditional Love grow in my heart,
Give my life a chance for a new, loving start.

I chose to be in the Light, to love everyone,
To share unconditional love under the sun.
So, I'll leave this dark, cancerous place.
Replacing ugly fear with Light and loving grace.

Nothing happens to me, my life's not a losing fight.
Everything happens through me—through my loving Light.
I am One in the Light, and the Light is One in me.
The Light is Life's Joy, its Joy heals me and sets me free.

CHAPTER **15**

What If I Could Meet Me Again?

THERE I WAS, SUSPENDED IN THE MIDDLE OF A GIGANTIC SPHERE, reviewing all of the events of my many lifetimes...instantly recalling all of the decisions in each and every episode. I was actually reliving my experiences, but doing it in a strange and detached way. I knew I was reliving individual events in my life, but simulateounsly, I was aware of the total life experience. It was like watching a movie I had previously seen. I knew how it ended, but still treasured seeing each individual part of the whole movie from the beginning.

〜〜〜〜〜〜

I woke up from a sound sleep and felt restless. *What now?* I thought. There were no phrases or thoughts spinning around in my mind, just an urge to get up and start writing. The only problem I could see was that I didn't know what to write.

As I sat at my desk staring at a blank sheet of paper, a series of thoughts immediately came to me. Knowing what I now know about my life, what would I say to me at certain stages of my life spanning the last seven decades? How

REMEMBERING THE LIGHT THROUGH PROSETRY*

would I mentor me, knowing the results of my many decisions throughout my life? What would I say to me if I could meet me again?

There in the quiet of the early morning I began to relive my life. I could actually feel the emotions at the various stages of my development here on earth. I remembered that most of the time I was filled with a fear of some kind. I was always looking for approval from those around me, rather than becoming the person I really knew I wanted to be.

So, I sat down and relived my life in my mind. I had an opportunity to go back in time and be a mentor to myself. I told the younger version of me what was really important as I remembered the various stages of my life.

Now, through the poem that was created before my eyes, I knew what to say to me—if I could meet me again throughout my life's journey.

WHAT IF I COULD MEET ME AGAIN?

If I Could Meet Me Again

If I could meet me again throughout my life,
In moments of joy, happiness, or strife
What would I say to this child, boy, or man,
To infuse my wisdom into his personal plan?

If I met me as a child at his mother's side,
Clutching her dress, keeping pace with her stride
I'd tell him to let go of his fear of being lost,
That a life filled with anxiety isn't worth the cost.

If I met me as a youngster just starting school,
Alone for the first time—feeling like a fool
I'd say learning is a wonderful way to life's start,
It builds self-confidence and a loving heart.

If I met me as a kid struggling with his art,
Thinking he's not good enough to set himself apart
I'd assert that creativity is a personal gift from above,
It's a worthwhile struggle overflowing with love.

If I met me as an adolescent unable to fit in
Growing into manhood, struggling with sin
I'd affirm that God loves without strings attached,
Life is built on choices—judgment is detached.

If I met me as a young man starting a career
Focusing on mistakes, driven by his fear
I'd declare that there is no wrong decision,
His work contributes to his life's mission.

◄ REMEMBERING THE LIGHT THROUGH PROSETRY*

If I met me as a husband living with his wife
Adjusting to a relationship void of his past life
I'd whisper love doesn't happen, it requires work,
Love her body, mind, and soul—don't be a jerk.

If I met me as a father choosing firmness over love
Struggling to discipline his three sons from above
I'd state that each one is different, each soul unique,
He has to let them go, if it's their love he seeks.

If I met me as an old man with a finite number of days
Looking for his next life, searching through the haze
I'd shout, death isn't final—filled with pain and fright,
He's returning to eternity to be One with the Light.

CHAPTER 16

Who Am I—Really?

ONE NIGHT I WOKE UP ABOUT TWO A.M. and was plagued with a question that wouldn't let me sleep. The question was, "Who am I? Who am I, really?" I knew all of the obvious, external characteristics of me, but was that the real me?

Tossing and turning for a while my mind went back to the day I drowned. At the moment of drowning I was very much alone, freezing cold, and filled with terror of my impending death. I wasn't contemplating "Who am I?" at that time.

And then the miracle happened. I remembered leaving my body and being pulled into the Light; and in that very instant I knew "who I really am!" I remembered that I am a piece of the Light, a piece of the holographic Universe, and a piece of the cosmic Oneness. I knew that I am more than my body, my mind, or my thoughts—I am actually the space between my thoughts.

I couldn't stay in bed. I had to get up and write down all of the images flashing through my thoughts. And so once more, I

◄ REMEMBERING THE LIGHT THROUGH PROSETRY*

found myself at my desk transcribing to paper the conceptual visions that were flooding my mind.

I finished the poem and immediately went back to sleep. The next morning I looked at the poem I had written and smiled as I read "Who Am I?"

Who Am I?

I am the silent space,
Existing between my thoughts.

I am infinite awareness,
Residing in my silent space.

I am unconditional love,
Vibrating through every breath.

I am continuous acceptance,
Embracing myself and all others.

I am spontaneous joy,
Overwhelming each and every moment.

I am eternal peace,
Experiencing the holographic universe.

I am unending gratitude,
Expressing gratefulness for my reality.

I am universal knowledge,
Releasing myself into the expanding cosmos.

I am unblemished truth,
Shining forth through the Light.

I am a piece of the Light,
Illuminating my Oneness from within the Light.

I am the silent space,
Existing between my thoughts.

CHAPTER 17

And I'm Remembering Again

WHEN I HEARD "ANDY, DON'T BE AFRAID," "Andy, I love you," and "Andy, we love you," I felt my whole body being absorbed into the Light—I became One with the Light. My awareness expanded such that I was in all the places in the Universe at the same moment. But, even as I expanded to encompass the Universe, I was still Andy, which is to say I never lost my "Andy-ness." What a phenomenon!

The Light was surrounded by a sea of other Lights. And as I gazed upon them I recognized them as billions of other souls, or pieces of Light. They were present to celebrate my return home—to become One with all of them.

While I was in and of the Light, my whole being opened up into the entire Universe. I knew I was home again. It was incredible to be in the Light again. I was elated being with all of the other billions of pieces of Light again. Not one of my earthly fears existed in the Light. I was completely and emotionally detached from all my previous negative thoughts, feelings, and experiences. I was filled with an unconditional

◄ REMEMBERING THE LIGHT THROUGH PROSETRY*

love, which had no bounds or limitations—it was all-encompassing. I was completely open to the Light, and the Light was completely open to me. We were all One.

It became apparent to me, after years of thinking about my NDE, that what I originally thought was a learning process for me on earth was actually a remembering process.

When I was in the Light I "knew" everything. I remember the sensation of knowing all there is to know in the Universe. It was as if I exploded and expanded into an infinite, knowing being. I knew it all. And as soon as I recognized that, there wasn't anything I didn't know. I smiled because I knew I was one with the Light.

One night, a few years ago, I woke up from a sound sleep with the phrase "and I remember" spinning around in my mind. No matter how I tried, I could not sleep. I had to write and as I did I began to remember again. My return to sleep was immediate as soon as I completed the poem.

A few hours later I read the poem and as I did so I remembered my journey into the Light as if it had just happened moments ago.

AND I'M REMEMBERING AGAIN

And I Remember

I remember ... I am a unique piece of the Light.
And I remember ... we all are unique pieces of the Light.
And I remember ... the Light is unconditional love.
And I remember ... the Light is unconditional acceptance.
And I remember ... we are All One.

I remember ... nothing matters—nothing really matters.
And I remember ... there is nothing that I have to do.
And I remember ... nothing ever happens to me.
And I remember ... everything always happens through me.
And I remember ... we are All One.

I remember ... I came back to recreate my realities anew.
And I remember ... I chose to forget the Light.
And I remember ... I chose to remember the Light again.
And I remember ... I can be whatever I choose to be.
And I remember ... we are All One.

I remember ... everything is a vibrating string of Energy.
And I remember ... I am a unique frequency of Light Energy.
And I remember ... we are all variations of Light Energy.
And I remember ... there is only one Light Energy.
And I remember ... we are All One in the Light.

CHAPTER **18**

How Does It Feel To Be Back?

IT HAD BEEN QUITE AWHILE since I woke up in the middle of the night with images and phrases churning in my head. But, last night it happened again. I was awakened by a repeating question, "How does it feel being back from the Light?" It was as if I were shouting to myself from the center of my mind. "How does it feel being back from the Light?" Over and over again, it wouldn't stop. I didn't want to get up, I was still very tired, but it felt like invisible hands were taking hold of me and wrenching me out of bed. I had no other choice. I had to get up.

So, I grabbed a couple of sheets of paper and a pen and started to write. I finished in less than an hour, and then I put it aside and went back to bed.

In a few hours I awoke and read "How Does It Feel?" The poem brought back all of the years of sadness, confusion, and anxiety that I endured immediately after my NDE. I did not want to come back to earth. It took half a lifetime for me to remember that my life here on earth is just an illusion anyway. I truly am a piece of the Light and I'll be returning soon.

◄ REMEMBERING THE LIGHT THROUGH PROSETRY*

How Does It Feel?

How does it feel …
Being back from the Light
Returned to this Earth
After being in a wondrous flight?

How does it feel …
To be One with the Light
And then stuffed back into a body
Filled with pain, fear, and fright?

How does it feel …
To know that life's an illusion
That we're lying and killing each other
In a state of hysterical confusion?

How does it feel …
Unable to describe the joy my heart hears
Of unconditional love and acceptance
To people consumed with hatred and fears?

How does it feel …
Being a stranger in a strange land
Confined by living in dimensions three
After holding the universe in the palm of my hand?

How does it feel …
Spending a lifetime alone
Staring into the eyes of others
Knowing they can't remember their Home?

HOW DOES IT FEEL TO BE BACK?

How does it feel …
Waiting for death to release me
Back into the Light of indescribable love
Totally absorbed by the infinite Sea?

How does it feel …
Being stuck on earth for all these years?
Disillusioned—yet joyful, knowing that soon
I'll return to the Light without fears.

CHAPTER 19

Death And The Light

AS I REVIEWED MY MANY LIVES IN THE ETERNAL NOW SPHERE, it became obvious to me that I was creating specific, unique realities. I could see myself in all of the variations of life in those three-dimensional planes. I could review and relive my many lives as a victim, a villain, or a co-creator. I observed all of the joys and sorrows I created. I comprehended each and every one of them.

I remembered the transitions between all of my lives were somehow mysteriously connected to one another. One life experience blended into another, and that one into yet another one—a continuum that defied rationale thinking, yet to me was completely understandable.

One of the greatest gifts that I received from my NDE was to never fear my earth-death again. I know death is just a transition from one multidimensional existence to another. And I also know that, at the moment of death, all of the pain, terror, agony, suffering, and horror is instantaneously replaced with a warm, unconditionally loving Light—and a joy that knows no bounds.

◄ REMEMBERING THE LIGHT THROUGH PROSETRY*

A dream about death. I woke up in the middle of the night from a dream about death. It was a pleasant dream. My dream was about how my understanding of and feelings about death had changed during my lifetime. In my dream I actually looked forward to my earth-death, not in a morbid or negative way, but in a loving way—loving the transition from being earthbound to becoming infinitely free.

I turned around and tried to go back to sleep, but the words "a love poem to death" kept swimming around in my mind. That seemed like a strange phrase, but the more I thought about it, the more it made sense to me. Death and birth are at the opposite ends of the earth experience, so why shouldn't both events be joyful. After tossing and turning for about an hour, it was obvious I couldn't go back to sleep, so I got up and tried to meditate.

Usually by the time I finish my mid-night meditation, I become very sleepy, but this night was different. I was energized. I felt an urge to write, to allow the myriad thoughts become more concrete.

The result was my writing "A Love Poem To Death."

DEATH AND THE LIGHT

A Love Poem To Death

When I was young I was taught to fear
Many things I now hold dear.
Strangers, failure, uncertainty, the dark,
The unknown, death, and alone in the park.

They said never question any unknown
I was afraid to think when I was alone.
And the greatest fear in my early life,
The black hole of death—ending my strife.

Oh, how I prayed to the righteous God
To save me from hell with a simple nod.
And take me to heaven where I could be glad,
Providing the good outnumbered the bad.

Then it happened, in only one take
I drowned at the bottom of an ice-cold lake.
I screamed, I choked, I breathed no more,
I let go and flew through death's open door.

In an instant, the smallest measure of time
I was infused with a love completely sublime.
The fear of my death melted away,
I was one with the Light, forever and a day.

I remember my earth-death, it's very, very clear
Void of all suffering, the Light is ever near.
Filled with love from the moment I let go,
My soul vanished from the mud down below.

◄ REMEMBERING THE LIGHT THROUGH PROSETRY*

My fear of death is replaced with love
I realized death is a transition from above.
Death released my soul from the shackles of earth,
Returning to the Light—my eternal rebirth.

As I remember, I have a smile on my face
Death returns me to a glorious place.
Infused completely with unconditional love,
Becoming One with the entire Universe above.

CHAPTER 20

Finally, Returning To The Light

I CAN'T SLEEP TONIGHT. I woke up four times, and it's still the middle of the night. Then I realize why I am restless. I haven't written the last poem for this book. The poem is to be titled "Return To The Light."

As I was writing this poem, I was filled with feelings of both joy and melancholy. It has been years since my NDE, and the older I get, the greater the ache and longing in my heart to go back home again. Don't get me wrong, I do love my life here on earth, but it is like a small, flickering candle placed on the surface of the sun, when compared to the boundless life I encountered in the Light.

So, as I began to write, my memory was flooded with images. Different images, of my absorption into the Light, flashed in front of my mind's eye as I wrote each verse.

I have been continually amazed that after many years, my recollections of my being in the Light have never varied.

◄ REMEMBERING THE LIGHT THROUGH PROSETRY*

Not one segment of those memories has been forgotten or enhanced. They are always, always remembered with the same acute details every time they pop into my mind. I always smile as those memories of the cosmic Light overwhelm me with love and peace as I begin to write the verses that are dancing in my mind.

As my life here on earth
Approaches its chronological end,
I reevaluate my earthly existence
Each event, every friend.
I remember being in the Light,
Into the cosmos I did ascend.

I will always remember the transition from my earth body into my Light body. It occurred in less than a blink of an eye. One moment I was consumed by the unbearable terror and pain of being stuck in the mud at the bottom of a lake, and in the next instant I was completely transformed—warm, happy, smiling, loving, and completely at peace. Wow, I am still astonished at how quickly and completely my transfiguration into the Light occurred. The closest feeling that I can recall here on earth happened when I was a young child. I became lost and couldn't find my mother. I was terrified. After crying and screaming for what seemed like hours to me, I finally found her and ran up into her arms. The instant she hugged me, I rejoiced because I knew I was safe and at home in my mother's arms. Those feelings are, in a small way, similar to what I felt when I was welcomed home and hugged in the arms of the Light.

FINALLY, RETURNING TO THE LIGHT

*I was ecstatic in the Light
Transcended from terror and pain,
Into a universe of warmth and love
An existence where bliss and joy reign.
Accepted unconditionally by the Light
Into its Oneness I did remain.*

I was raised in a family and atmosphere that were fear-based. I lived in constant fear of doing something wrong and then being punished for all eternity. In the Light there is no judgment, condemnation, or fear—only unconditional love and acceptance. Do you know how liberating it is to remember that in the unending Universe, there is only the love of the Light? Oh, how the Light and I laughed and smiled at how silly I was to spend so much of my earthly life in sadness and fear. The Light enabled me to remember that although I came to earth to experience both love and fear, I did not go to earth to be dominated by fear. I went for the experience of choosing love over fear.

*I reviewed all my lifetimes
No judgment, condemnation, or fear.
My earthly interactions with others
Rendered laughter, sorrow, and tears.
My choices were acknowledged by the Light
We relived each one suspended in a sphere.*

What was it like being fused into the Light? It was like

◀ REMEMBERING THE LIGHT THROUGH PROSETRY*

my last exhale; it was like releasing my grip on my three-dimensional life; it was like finally letting go of every fearful thought. And it all happened in the same moment of eternity. The ecstasy, peace, and joy became more than feelings. They actually became "the me" that was fused into the Light. Liberation and freedom transformed into my eternal breath, because nothing (no thing) was unknown to me. It was like floating in the sea of complete knowledge.

Fused into the Light of Oneness
Submerged in waters of unconditional love.
Ecstasy, peace, and joy all-consuming
Transformed into infinite dimensions above.
Nothing hidden, nothing unknown
Traversing galaxies on the wings of a dove.

When I was in the Light I thought I was home forever. "Not so," said the Light. "Andy, you must go back!" It was the sound of terror in paradise. No, I wouldn't, I couldn't go back into that pain-laden, broken, severely limited, earthly body. Never!

I was wrong.

One moment I was immersed in the unconditional love of the Light, and in the very next instant I was stuffed, kicking and screaming, back into the body that was recovered from the bottom of the lake. Oh my God, how sad I was. How sad I still am. How horrible it was to be back on earth, with all its limitations. I am a child who can't find my moth-

FINALLY, RETURNING TO THE LIGHT

er again, and the search goes on, unsuccessfully, for the rest of my earthly life. I'm lost and I can't find my way back home.

> *In the midst of my splendor, my rhapsody*
> *Sent back to earth unhappy and sad.*
> *Out of the Light, confused and afraid*
> *Roaming the world like a displaced nomad.*
> *Trying to understand why I'm back*
> *Makes me feel awkward, lost, and unclad.*

The first 20 years after my NDE were some of the saddest in my earthly life. I wandered the world as a true nomad. I don't even know what I was searching for. I was haunted by memories that never changed and never went away. I was afraid to talk about my Light experience with anyone because I thought I was crazy and I knew they would think I was crazy too. I felt if I ever told anyone about my earth-death experience, I would probably be put away in an asylum.

Finally, in 1976, I stumbled across a book about Near Death Experiences. *Life After Life*, by Dr. Raymond Moody.

Yes! My Near Death Experience was real. It is real. I can smile again—I am not crazy. From that day on, my life was immediately filled with a joyful knowing that my NDE memories were true, and I would never be fearful again.

◄ REMEMBERING THE LIGHT THROUGH PROSETRY*

Earthly days pass slowly in sadness
I resolve not to remember or stay.
Random acts of joy fill my life
Memories of the Light will not go away.
Smiles appear in my face, heart, and soul
As Light's vibrating love consumes each day.

So, now I am waiting with a smile on my face. I'll be going back home soon. And I remember the instant I was welcomed by the Light—every earthly action, reaction, feeling, and experience didn't matter anymore. The only thing that mattered to the Light, and to me, was my choice to accept and love unconditionally. This choice brought smiles on the face of the Light—this choice brought smiles on my eternal face. What does it mean for me to go home again, to go back into the Light? It means I'll be released from the shackles of a three-dimensional, fear-based, earthly confinement and smile again—with the Light for all eternity.

When my life here on earth
Attains its chronological end
Consumed by unconditional love
The Light promised to send.
Earthly memories quickly fade away
Into the Light my soul transcends.

FINALLY, RETURNING TO THE LIGHT

Return To The Light

*As my life here on earth
Approaches its chronological end,
I reevaluate my earthly existence
Each event, every friend.
I remembered being in the Light,
Into the cosmos I did ascend.*

*I was ecstatic in the Light
Transcended from terror and pain,
Into a universe of warmth and love
An existence where bliss and joy reign.
Accepted unconditionally by the Light
Into its Oneness I did remain.*

*I reviewed all my lifetimes
No judgment, condemnation, or fear.
My earthly interactions with others
Rendered smiles, laughter, sorrow, and tears.
All my choices acknowledged by the Light
We relived each one suspended in a sphere.*

*Fused into the Light of Oneness
Submerged in waters of unconditional love.
Ecstasy, peace, and joy all-consuming
Transformed into infinite dimensions above.
Nothing hidden, nothing unknown
Traversing galaxies on the wings of a dove.*

◄ REMEMBERING THE LIGHT THROUGH PROSETRY*

In the midst of my splendor, my rhapsody
Sent back to earth unhappy and sad.
Out of the Light, confused and afraid
Roaming the world like a displaced nomad.
Trying to understand why I'm back
Makes me feel awkward, lost, and unclad.

Earthly days pass slowly in sadness
I resolve not to remember or stay.
Random acts of joy fill my life
Memories of the Light will not go away.
Smiles appear in my face, heart, and soul
As Light's vibrating love consumes each day.

When my life here on earth
Attains its chronological end.
Consumed by unconditional love
The Light promised to send.
Earthly memories quickly fade away
As into the Light my soul transcends.

Epilogue

I'M JUST A REGULAR GUY who happened to drown, die, and then return to earth. I am able to remember what happened to me while I was earth-dead. When I returned from my earth-death, I was not given any instructions, missions, or tasks to tell others about my encounter with the Light. In fact, I had no idea what in the hell had just happened. I was frightened and very sad for many years.

I chose (after more than 20 years of anguish) to finally share my remembrances. So, that is all I do when people ask me about my NDE—I *share* my NDE remembrances. And sharing is the only reason for this book. It enables me to describe my adventures with the infinite through prose and poetry—prose and poetry, which have never come *from* me, but have always come *through* me...from the Light in the middle of the night.

Since my awareness and understanding of my NDE, I strive to live my life on earth with unconditional acceptance and love. Every decision to love ignites glorious memories of the Light within me. Unconditional love is a personal choice. I personally choose to love unconditionally, which means I

◄ REMEMBERING THE LIGHT THROUGH PROSETRY*

don't have any demands or expectations from anyone—including myself.

When I was in the Light I knew that life on planet earth was just an illusion—truly a grand illusion—but an illusion nonetheless. There is only One Light, and we are all pieces of that One Light.

Peace, love, and joy to all from the One Light.

Lightning Source UK Ltd.
Milton Keynes UK
UKOW02f1044260515

252282UK00001B/246/P